GW01605407

From Mr. and Mrs. Bond. Christmas 1982.

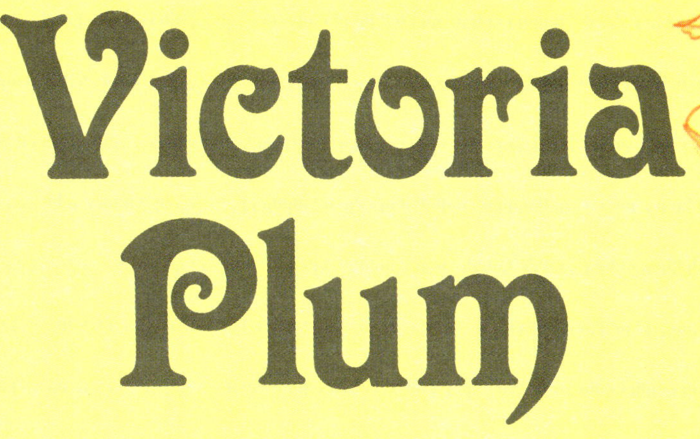

Victoria Goes Fishing

Angela Rippon

PURNELL

SBN 361 05061 5
Text copyright © 1981 Daredevils Limited
Illustrations copyright © 1981 Purnell and Sons Limited
'Victoria Plum' copyright © 1981 W.N. Sharpe Limited
Published 1980 by Purnell Books, Berkshire House, Queen Street, Maidenhead, Berkshire
Made and printed in Great Britain by Purnell and Sons Limited, Paulton (Bristol) and London

Victoria Plum looked out of the window at the bright sun and the clear blue sky and decided it was far too nice a day to stay indoors. She daydreamed about lying in the hot sun, paddling her toes in the cool, clear river.

"Are you daydreaming, Victoria?" The deep voice of her teacher brought Victoria back to earth with a bump. She was not out in the sunshine after all, but sitting at a desk piled high with school books, and a rather cross-looking teacher was standing in front of her.

"It's no good wishing you could be outside when there is work to be done," he said, and then he smiled to show that he was not very cross. "The sooner we finish, the sooner we can enjoy this lovely day," he added, "so let's hurry on." With that he balanced his spectacles on the end of his nose, and started reading aloud from one of his huge, old books.

Although everyone in the Great Wood called Victoria Plum a woodland fairy, she was only a very junior fairy, and still had many things to learn before she could become a real fairy with a full set of magic wings.

Every week Victoria and her friend Benjamin, who was a woodland elf, went to the home of the old alchemist to learn all they could about magic. He was one of the oldest gnomes in the Great Wood and knew more about magic than anyone else there. He had once lived in the fairy kingdom, and had worked on some of the fairies' most important spells.

Usually Victoria loved to listen to his stories about the most famous fairies and the bravest gnomes, but today it was too hot and she could not concentrate on anything. At last the old man put down his book and looked at them over the top of his little gold spectacles.

"I'm going to teach you two how to disappear," he said in a very serious voice. Victoria and Ben could not believe their ears. They both knew that only the most senior fairies could make things disappear, and they were very junior fairies. It would be years before they had enough magic to cast such an important spell as that.

"We cannot possibly do that," gasped Victoria. "We are not nearly clever enough." The old man just smiled at them.

"What you must remember," he said, "is that you do not always need magic to get what you want. Sometimes you can do the cleverest things without using magic at all!" Ben and Victoria were still puzzled. Then they saw that he was not just smiling, he was chuckling, then laughing.

"Why don't you both disappear?" he said. "Go home. Go out into the wood and enjoy the sunshine. That's how you make yourselves disappear without using magic. Perhaps at your next lesson we can get some work done." Victoria and Ben did not wait to hear any more. They gathered up their books, said a hurried goodbye and disappeared from the room and out into the lazy heat of the lovely summer day.

Ben ran all the way to the bend in the path before he stopped, in case the old gnome changed his mind and called them back. "He's not such a bad stick after all," said Ben. "Fancy letting us have the whole day off! It's great." Ben started to play a tune on his pipes to let the whole wood know how pleased he was to have the rest of the day to himself to do what he liked.

As they walked on through the trees a bumble bee flew overhead. Her legs were covered with sacs of pollen, and it looked as though she was wearing yellow trousers.

"Why are you dashing about on a day like this?" asked Ben. "Slow down and relax." The bee hovered for a moment.

"Buzz. Buzz," she said. "We have to work even harder when the sun shines," and she dived into another flower. When she came out she was covered in golden pollen grains.

"You look like a big yellow powder puff," laughed Victoria. The busy bumble bee was not amused.

"Have you nothing better to do?" she asked rather crossly. Ben and Victoria both shook their heads.

"We are having the whole day off," they replied.

"I've been so buzzzy collecting pollen that my feet have hardly touched the ground," said the bee. "All the bees are hard at work so that we can make lots of honey." Just then she saw a flower she had not visited. "Must dash," she said and flew off back to work.

"It wears me out to listen to her," laughed Ben.

They walked on down the path which ran through the trees to the edge of a small river. Victoria could hear it happily chuckling and gurgling over the stones, and as they drew nearer she could see the sun glinting and sparkling on the water through the trees.

"Let's have a paddle," said Victoria, and before Ben had time to say a word she had flown down the path, put down her books, and was sitting on the grassy river bank, hurriedly pulling off her shoes and socks.

Victoria curled her toes in the cool water and decided that this was the perfect way to spend a summer day.

"I shall sit here in the warm sunshine on this smooth grassy bank and dangle my toes in the water for the rest of the day," she thought as she leaned back against a tree. She watched a cloud of small flies hovering above the river, busily turning this way and that as though they could not make up their minds where they were going. A dragonfly flashed by in a streak of brilliant blue on some urgent message, and the black and white dipper birds bobbed and curtsied impatiently on the rocks in the river.

When they called out to her, "What are you doing today, Victoria Plum?" the little woodland fairy just smiled and replied happily, "Nothing. Absolutely nothing. I am having a day off," and she closed her eyes so that everyone would think she was asleep, and would not disturb her.

Ben was dozing in the shade of a tree. Its branches stretched out over the river so that the leaves on the very tip danced on the surface of the water. They made a gentle burbling noise that helped him to sleep. Suddenly he and Victoria were startled by a loud splash. They both looked at the water and saw a long stream of silver bubbles. Then there was a whoosh of water, an even louder splash, and there sitting up on his hind legs in the middle of the river was a young otter.

"Hello," he said breathlessly. "I hope I did not startle you, but I can't remember when I've had to swim so fast," and he lay on his back in the water to catch his breath.

"Why is everybody rushing about?" asked Ben. "Why can't you have a day off like Victoria and me, and lie in the sun?" Otter cleaned his whiskers, scratched himself and said, "I was having a day off. I was lying in the sun – that's the trouble!" He gave his whiskers another comb with his soft paws. "There I was having a quiet snooze in a patch of sunlight when I was hit on the head with a stone." He pointed to a red bump on his head. "It hurts too," he said, rubbing it gently with his paw.

"Why would anyone want to throw stones at you?" asked Victoria, very surprised.

"Well," said Otter. "They were not actually throwing stones at me, they were throwing them at a tin can, but they missed the can and hit me instead."

"Who are they?" asked Ben. Otter twitched his whiskers.

"Them," he said. "Those children from the village. They have come down to the river to fish, but they were bored and started throwing stones instead. I don't think they saw me, but I was not going to hang around to find out," and he dived under the water to show how quickly he could disappear when he chose to. When he popped his head up again he said, "All the young fish are terrified. They want to swim further down the river but they dare not go past the children in case they are caught on their fishing hooks." Otter shivered at the thought of the fishing hooks, and then darted under the water again as if to escape. When he came up by the edge of the bank Victoria smiled at him and said, "Tell me where the children are, Otter. We must think of some way to stop them catching all those young fish."

"They are on the far side of the river by the deep pool," replied Otter, "but please do not ask me to come back with you. I am not very brave, and I don't like meeting people," and he looked at Victoria with such big sad eyes that Victoria said she was sure that she and Ben could manage on their own. Ben was not sure at all, but Victoria was already flying across the top of the water and heading for the deep pool.

"Ah well," sighed Ben. "I had better be off too," and he flew after Victoria.

Victoria soon found the children sitting on the bank laughing, all saying that they would be the first to catch a fish. She looked into the deep pool and could see the young fish swimming round in circles. They were frightened to swim past the children in case they were caught, but they did not want to stay in the deep pool. "What shall we do, Victoria?" they cried. Victoria sat on the bank and thought hard. Very soon Ben arrived. "All right," he said. "What marvellous scheme have you come up with this time?" Victoria shook her head sadly, for she had not worked out any plan at all. She knew that neither she nor Ben had enough magic to make the children go away, though that was what she wanted them to do. While Victoria went on thinking, Ben flew over to the other side of the pool to have a closer look at the children. He flew right in front of their noses and watched them put fresh pieces of bread on their fishing lines. They could not see Ben, of course, for although the woodland creatures can see the fairies, they are almost always invisible to humans. Ben soon flew back to Victoria again. "They are a useless bunch," he said. "If you ask me, even if they did catch a fish they would not know the difference between a trout and an old boot." Victoria jumped up as if she had been stuck with a pin. "Ben, you are clever," she cried. "You've found the answer straight away!"

"I only said they could not tell the difference between a trout and an old boot," said Ben. "Exactly," replied Victoria. "Remember what our teacher told us this morning. He said you can do the cleverest things without using magic at all." Ben nodded doubtfully. "It's simple," said Victoria. "We don't want the children to catch the fish so we give them something else to catch – like old boots!" At last Ben understood the plan. "We'll have to use a bit of magic," said Victoria, "just to persuade them that they are catching something special."

Victoria put her hand into her pocket and brought out some fairy dust. "I had this left over from today's lesson," she said. She flew across to the children, sprinkled fairy dust in their eyes and chanted a secret fairy spell. Then she flew back to Ben. "Now for stage two of the plan," she said.

"I was supposed to be having a day off," grumbled Ben.

"I know," replied Victoria, "but this could be much more fun. All you have to do is fly along the river bank and collect all the rubbish you can find, and then we'll work a spell to make sure the children catch it on their lines." Ben still did not look very happy. "Look," said Victoria. "There is an old rusty kettle and a bicycle wheel. They will do for a start, but I'm sure you will be able to find something much more interesting."

Ben could never resist a challenge.

"You bet I can," he said, and flew off to search.

Very carefully and very quietly Victoria put the kettle in the water so that it did not splash. Then she watched as it drifted towards the fishing lines. The handle caught in one of the hooks and pulled the line tight. "We've caught something," the children shouted, and they wound in the line and found the kettle dangling on the end. Victoria kept her fingers crossed and hoped that her spell had worked. If it had not, she knew that the children would throw the kettle back into the river and wait until they caught a fish. As she watched, they began to laugh and clap their hands with delight. "What a smashing bit of treasure," cried one. "I've never caught a kettle fish before!" laughed another. The third said, "I wonder what other treasure we can catch," and he threw his line back into the water to see what else he could find. Almost at once he caught the old bicycle wheel. "I've caught another treasure," he shouted, and as he pulled in the line the wheel slowly came out of the pool. The bright summer sun sparkled on all the tiny drops of water that clung to the rim and the spokes of the wheel. One of the children shouted, "Look. It's all covered in fairy lights," and Victoria had a little chuckle to herself. "Little do you know," she thought. Then she watched as the children pulled in the bicycle wheel, and put it with the battered old kettle on the river bank.

While the three children were examining their finds, Ben flew back to the deep pool. "It's all arranged, Victoria," he said. "I've found loads of rubbish lying around on the river bank. You would never believe the things some people throw away. It should keep the children amused for hours." Ben was quite right. After the wheel, the children caught an old felt hat. It was battered and soaking wet, but they put it out in the sun to dry and then went on with their fishing. Next they caught a small, green glass bottle, and then a saucepan to go with the kettle, and then a huge white plastic bag, and lots of other things as well. Every time they pulled one thing off their fishing hooks, Victoria and Ben dropped something else into the water a little way upstream, so that by the end of the morning the children had a large collection of treasures piled on the bank beside them.

At last the children thought they had caught enough. One of them picked up the hat, which was now nice and dry, and put it on his head. Another put the saucepan on his head and hung the kettle over his arm. The third boy picked up the plastic bag, carefully put the rest of their catch inside, and slung it over his shoulder. The boy wearing the felt hat picked up the bicycle wheel and began bowling it along the woodland path.

"I'll race you home," he shouted, and they all chased after him through the trees.

When everything was quiet, Ben and Victoria flew out into the middle of the pool to make sure the children had gone. Then they called down to the young fish who were still trying to hide in the shade of the river bank.

"It's all right, the children have gone. You can come out now. It's quite safe." One by one the fish poked their noses out into the deeper water in the centre of the pool. As they gradually grew braver, they swam into the warm sunlight, until at last they were all gathered in a silvery mass in the middle of the pool.

"Thank you, Victoria. Thank you, Ben," they gurgled under the water, and they swam round and round, chasing their tails with delight now that they knew they were safe.

After a while they began to swim out into the river, and as they went they called back to Victoria and Ben,

"We'll never forget you, and we will come and see you when we swim back to this part of the river." Victoria and Ben knew it might be years before they saw the young fish again, and that when they did return they would have grown into large and handsome fish.

"Remember where we live," called Victoria. As she waved goodbye to them she watched their silver bodies streak through the water as they chased each other over the stones and between the reeds down the river.

"So much for my day off," laughed Ben. "I think I'll go before any more work turns up."

Ben gathered up his books and his pipes, said goodbye to Victoria and whizzed off back to his house for some tea.

Victoria picked up her school books from the ground and was just about to fly home for tea herself when something on the far bank caught her eye. It was a sudden flash of green light which seemed to come from the long grass.

"Whatever was that?" she thought, and flew over to investigate. There on the ground she saw a lovely green glass bottle that the children had fished out of the river. They had carried away in their big bag all the other treasures they had caught on their lines, but the bottle was so tiny that they had not noticed it lying in the grass, and had left it behind. Victoria picked up the bottle and held it towards the sun so that the light flashed and danced inside the tiny bottle like green fire.

"This is much too beautiful to leave lying around," she thought, "and I know just the place for it." She took the bottle home and put it on the window sill in her bedroom. It made a perfect vase for a bunch of crisp, white daisies, and in the mornings, when the sun shone through the window, the little green bottle caught the sunbeams and looked as though it was full of sparkling green lights.

"I'm so glad we let the children fish for treasure," thought Victoria, "because they left me the best treasure of all."